W9-BII-573

GUYS' GUIDES

Chillin'

A Guy's Guide to Friendship

By Michael Sommers

the rosen publishing group's
rosen central
new york

Published in 2000 by The Rosen Publishing Group, Inc.
29 East 21st Street, New York, NY 10010

First Edition

Library of Congress Cataloging-in-Publication Data

Sommers, Michael A., 1966
    Chillin' : a guy's guide to friendship / by Sommers, Michael.—1st ed.
      p. cm. — (Guys' guides)
    Includes bibliographical references and index.
    Summary: Provides advice on making new friends and negotiating issues such as peer pressure, acceptance, and conformity.
    ISBN 0-8239-3160-9
    1. Friendship in adolescence　Juvenile literature. 2. Teenage boys—Psychology　Juvenile literature. [1. Friendship.] I. Title. II. Series.
BF725.3.F64S66 1999
158.2'5'08351—dc21

                                                99-41435
                                                CIP

Manufactured in the United States of America

>>> contents >>>

>> About this book <<

It's not easy being a guy these days. You're expected to be buff, studly, and masculine, but at the same time, you're supposed to be sensitive, thoughtful, and un-macho. And that's not all. You have to juggle all of this while you're wading through the shark-infested waters of middle school. So not only are you dealing with raging hormones, cliques, and geeks, and body changes, but you're also supposed to figure out how to be a Good Guy. As if anyone is even sure what that means anyway. It's enough to make you wish for the caveman days, when guys just grunted and wrestled mammoths with their bare hands and stuff.

Being an adolescent is complicated. Take girls, for example. Just five minutes ago—or so it seems—they weren't much different from you and your buddies. Now, suddenly you can't keep your eyes off them, and other parts of your body have taken an interest too. Or maybe you're not interested in girls yet, and you're worried about when you will be. Then there's figuring out where you fit into the middle school world. Are you a jock, a brain, or what? And how come it seems that someone else gets to decide for you? What's up with that?

Yeah, it's tough. Still, you're a smart guy, and you'll figure it all out. That's not to say that we can't all use a hand. That's where this book comes in. It's sort of a cheat sheet for all the big tests that your middle school years throw at you. Use it to help you get through the amazing maze of your life—and to come out alive on the other side.

<<<What Are Friends For?>>>

The Beatles summed it up pretty well in the 1960s when they recorded the song "I Get By with a Little Help from My Friends."

Sometimes friends can be tiresome. Other times they can be troublesome. But most of the time, friends are a heck of a lot of fun.

Because you were born into your family, you don't get to choose your brothers or sisters, your mom, or your dad. You do get to choose your friends.

This is pretty exciting, since it means that the whole world is full

of potential pals. Depending on how open you are, there is no limit to the variety of friends you can have. You can find friends who are older or younger than you are, kids or adults, guys or girls. You can have one-on-one friendships or hang out with a whole gang of buddies. Friends might live in your neighborhood, they might go to your school, or live in another country altogether. What's important is that you guys enjoy hanging out together, can say what you want to each other, can be yourselves with each other. All different types of people can be your friends. You can also have different kinds or levels of friendships.

By the Numbers

As you move into your teens, friends will become more and more important in your life. A recent study discovered that teens spend 29 percent of their waking time hanging out with pals. Meanwhile, parents spend only 7 percent of their time with adult friends.

Most guys have many casual friends. These are kids you know from class or say "hey" to in the hall. Many guys have a few closer pals with whom they sit in the cafeteria at lunch, watch a hockey game, or hang out on weekends.

If you're lucky, you'll also have a couple of really good, committed friends. These are pals whom you trust, with whom you can share your closest secrets and your biggest problems. Likewise, they can do the same with you. Such pals are pretty hard to come by. If you're lucky enough to have one (or more), hang on to him as if he were gold.

Good friends can comfort you when you're feeling down. They can counsel you when you have a problem and you need to talk to someone your own age who really understands. They can challenge you to try new things, to become a better person. Probably some of the best times you will have in your life will be moments spent with your buds.

<<<Making New Pals>>> 2

From time to time, many guys find themselves in situations where they are without friends. You might move to a new city or country or transfer from one school to another. You might be shy and have difficulty opening up to kids your own age. Or perhaps you have a physical difference—you're overweight, you speak with a stutter, you suffer from asthma, you use a wheelchair—that you feel sets you apart from those around you.

Guys in these situations may have some insecurities. They sometimes feel that nobody likes them. This is usually a mistake,

however. Kids, like adults, can sometimes react in a negative way to things and to people that are new or different. Probably it isn't that other kids don't like you; it's that they don't know you.

If you find yourself in a situation where you are new or different, of course you are going to feel a little nervous or self-conscious. But no matter how unsure you might feel, don't isolate yourself from everybody else. Let other kids get to know you—and like you.

>>How to Make New Pals<<

The key to making new friends is conversation. Talking is the way we reach out and connect to others.

The trick to starting a conversation and keeping it going is to ask questions. If you ask questions, you don't have to talk that much, you just have to listen. Surprisingly, a lot of kids say that a good listener is one of the best qualities to have in a friend.

"I'm kind of shy and I really suck at talking to new kids," says twelve-year-old Levon. "I kind of freeze up and can't think of anything to say."

>>Where to Make New Pals<<

Since you spend most of your life at school, it's pretty logical to begin looking for potential pals right there. Your classes are a good place to start. Right off the bat you'll have some stuff in common with classmates—such as subjects, teachers, homework, and stress. Just being in class with each other might not give you enough opportunity to hang out much, though. Suggest working together on a project or studying for a test together. Combine the work with something fun. Take a burger break or go for a bike ride with your new bud.

Another way to make pals at school is to participate in activities. If you like sports, join a team. Sports bring guys together, as they require that you play as a team and cooperate.

If sports aren't your thing, think about working on the school paper, auditioning for the play, or joining the choir or orchestra. If there is something you like to do that isn't offered at your school, you could always start up

a group or club yourself! Getting involved in activities like these will not only make you feel more self-confident but will also make you feel like a part of things.

Of course, even though you spend a lot of time at school, don't feel as if this has to be the only focus of your life. If you're having a tough time fitting in at school, there are other places to make friends. Maybe there are some cool kids in your neighborhood you could hang out with. If you look out the window and see a couple of guys tossing a Frisbee or hanging out on a front stoop, go up to them, introduce yourself, and ask if you can join them. Chances are they'll say "sure."

Another way to meet new friends is to get involved in an extracurricular activity. Choose something that really interests you—cooking, karate, painting, or fencing, for example. This way you're bound to meet kids with similar interests. Religious groups, youth associations, and scouting groups are also good ways to meet and hang out with guys your own age.

Even if you have a lot of buddies at school, there is nothing wrong with making pals outside of school, too. In fact, having different kinds of friends whom you know from different places and with whom you share various interests will make your life much more interesting. It also ensures that if you're having problems with one particular pal or group of pals, you'll have other buddies to hang out with until things blow over.

>>Being a Good Pal<<

Making friends can be a tricky process. Sometimes keeping them can be as well.

One of the easiest things to do is to take a friend for granted. It is also one of the worst things you can do. Like all good things, a friendship takes a certain amount of maintenance. You might love your brand-new dirt bike, but if you let the tires go flat, park it on the ground, and leave it out in the rain to rust, it's not going to last very long. Same deal with a friendship.

The Friendship Quiz

See if you've got what it takes to be a good pal. Take the following test to see how many good friendship traits you have. Answer each question by choosing (1) Hardly Ever; (2) Sometimes; (3) Almost Always.

ARE YOU:

Hardly Ever	Sometimes	Almost Always

Tolerant Do you let your pals have their own opinions, make their own decisions, and disagree with you?

Understanding Do you let it go when your buddy has a problem and he barks at you for no reason?

Reliable Do you show up on time if you planned to meet a friend at a specific time and place?

Open-Minded Put off what you want to do for another time if your pals are in the mood to do something else?

Trustworthy Do you control the urge to tell a secret or talk behind your buddy's back?

Sensitive Keep your A+ to yourself if your pal is upset because he got a D?

Loyal Would you start hanging out less with your old pals if the "in" crew at school starts paying attention to you?

Generous Do you do nice things for a pal even if it means not doing something for yourself?

Patient Do you let your friends talk about their problems even if you'd rather talk about something else?

Dependable Do you pay a pal back (without him asking) when you borrow cash from him and promise to pay it back?

Honest If a close friend asks you for your opinion, do you tell (a tactful version of) the truth instead of what you think he wants to hear?

Scoring:

For each "Hardly Ever" give yourself 1 point.
For each "Sometimes" give yourself 2 points.
For each "Almost Always" give yourself 3 points.

Add up your total score:

11 or less—Better shape up and start paying more attention to your buds.
12-22—Overall you're a fine friend, but you have some problem spots that you might like to work on.
23-33—You're a true prince of a pal.

<<<Hangin' Out>>>

3

Sometimes nothing beats kickin' back with the guys. Hangin' with guys your own age creates a special bond that is hard to find with anyone else. You guys are all going through the same things. You get off on the same jokes and like to blast the same tunes. You like (or can't stand) the same girls. You make up code names and inside jokes. You might have rituals like a Friday night card game or a Sunday morning basketball game. These are all events and moments that bind you together. Even if it's just about cracking up or chillin' out, to lead a healthy life, it's important to have times like these.

Hangin' with Their Homeys

Leo DiCaprio flies his posse of actor amigos Tobey Maguire, Lukas Haas, and Elijah Wood to whatever location he's working in—whether it's Florida or France.

Scotty Morris wanted to play music he really dug with guys he really dug—so he hooked up with his best buds, and they formed the band Bad Voodoo Daddy.

Dawson's Creek cohorts James Van Der Beek and Joshua Jackson are not only pals, they were also housemates in Wilmington, North Carolina, where the hit TV show is filmed.

>>Hangin' Loose<<

There are a lot of ways you can spend time with your buddies. You can sit around watching videos on TV, or you can hang out in the park. You can check out the action at the mall or go swimming at the local pool.

When you're hanging out with a whole group of people, you don't always get to do what you want. In some cases, majority rules. Sometimes it's good to follow others' suggestions. You can end up trying new things or meeting new people whom you wouldn't encounter on your own.

"I was kind of afraid of waterskiing," confesses thirteen-year-old Jack. "I knew a guy who wiped out really bad and spent the rest of his life in a wheelchair. When Vern, Pedro, and Manny all decided to go waterskiing on the lake, at first I made up an excuse not to go. But they kept bugging me. They said it wouldn't be the same without me and if I really didn't want to ski, I could just flake out on the beach. In the end, I did end up trying it—and it really rocked! I'm so glad I listened to those guys!"

>>Hangin' Tight<<

Other times, however, you should listen to your conscience. If you're not comfortable diving off the top diving board, going to a movie you know your parents don't want you to see, or throwing water balloons from the school roof— don't. Never do something all the other guys are doing just because all the other guys are doing it. Of course, it's fun to be one of the gang, but this doesn't mean that you have to be with the gang all the time and do everything they do.

It's one thing to compromise or try something new. It's quite another to do something you really don't want to do—especially if you know that it's wrong or harmful to yourself or someone else. If your buddies coax and whine and plead with you, be cool. Don't waste your breath giving long-winded excuses. Simply say, "Hey man, I'm just not interested."

If being around drugs or alcohol—or people who drink or do drugs—makes you uncomfortable, you have two options. One is not to go to parties where you suspect they might be. Another is to go, but to plan in advance how to react if drugs or alcohol are offered to you.

The key to saying no and not coming off as a goody-goody is your attitude. If your 'tude is a laid-back and confident, "This is what's right for me, but I'm not going to judge anybody else," then your peers will probably be pretty cool with your decision.

What's more important is that you're cool with your decision. You don't make real friends trying to impress people by being something you're not. You make real friends by being yourself.

<<<Fitting In>>>

4

No matter what the age, everybody wants to feel as if he's a part of things. When you're in middle school, a tremendous part of your life revolves around school and friends. This is a time when you begin to change—both physically and emotionally. As you become more independent and start to rely less directly on your parents, your life changes as well.

Most teens try to fit in. There's nothing wrong with that as long as the changes you make let you feel comfortable with yourself.

Some guys try too hard. They want so much to be accepted by others that they lose their own identity. They follow others even if it means doing something that they feel is wrong.

Some guys want friends so badly that they'll spend $120 on a pair of sneakers, get wasted drinking brewskies, or get beat up because they joined a street gang.

Other guys don't try at all. They tend to be loners who pretend not to care whether or not they are accepted by their peers. It's great to have the confidence to be different and assert your own individuality. But as the English poet John Donne said, "No man is an island."

>>Peer Pressure<<

Everybody at school—with the exception of the teachers— thought Jake, Denis, and Lamar were cool. Everybody knew who they were, and nobody wanted to mess with them. They wore the funkiest clothes, carried shiny switchblades, and always had some hot-looking girls hanging out with them.

Merle didn't have too many friends, but he got to know Denis when Mrs. Potter assigned them a project together. Merle didn't mind doing most of the work. He got really good grades easily, and Denis seemed to dig him big-time. He even invited

Merle to start hanging out with Jake and Lamar. Lots of times these guys cut class.

"Sitting in that boring classroom, we're missing out on a whole lotta life," explained Jake.

"Yeah, dude," said Lamar in a friendly voice. "Why don't you ditch class and hang with us?"

Merle really wanted to hang out with these guys. He hoped they'd ask him to join their posse, and then he'd be one of the cool dudes in school. At the same time, he still put a lot of effort into his schoolwork. He cut class once to hang out at the mall. Then he cut another time to sit around drinking beer in Jake's dad's van. The second time he cut class, he missed a surprise math quiz and ended up with a zero.

"Who cares, man?" laughed Denis, when he told them. "What's a little quiz compared to having fun and enjoying life?" When he said that, Merle was kind of pissed off. For the first time, he asked himself if any of his new pals would feel bad for him if he flunked out of school because he cut classes with them.

"No, they wouldn't," he thought to himself.

Peer pressure is when people try to persuade you to do something that "everybody else" is doing and that they think you should do too. The bottom line on peer pressure is that a true friend would never try to make you do something you don't want to do. If you feel that you're having trouble standing up to peer pressure about something, ask yourself this: Will the people who are putting pressure on you take the consequences of your actions for you? If your grades start to suffer, for example, who is going to pay the price—you or them?

Cool Quotes

"I was always the kid who was a little odd. In high school, people didn't understand me. I wish I knew back then what I know now—that it's better to be different."
—actor Nicolas Cage

>>Popularity<<

According to the dictionary, a "popular" person means someone who is "widely liked by friends, associates, or acquaintances and sought after for company."

At school the "popular" kids are the cool kids everybody seems to like, everybody wants to be like, and by whom everybody wants to be liked. "Unpopular" kids are the nerdy kids whom everyone seems to ignore, pick on, and dis. Remember, though, many unpopular kids are smart and talented. In the end, a lot of what makes some kids popular is nothing more than surface appeal or image.

Nobody's going to say that popularity doesn't have its perks. Popular kids are usually liked not only by other kids but by teachers and parents as well. Popular kids get lots of attention. They seem to have an easier time making friends.

But take a look at some kids at your school who are "popular." Are they really popular in the sense that everybody likes them? Maybe they're just popular in the sense that everybody knows who they are because they have a certain look or style.

Popular kids aren't "winners," and less popular kids aren't "losers." Usually it's just that popular kids are attractive in a conventional way and appeal to a lot of people. "Conventional" means something that represents the standard or norm.

Cool Quotes

"Forget about trying to fit in. It's okay to look a little quirky. Now I realize those handsome same-looking guys are a dime a dozen. I'm the kind of guy people remember. In high school I hated that idea. But now it gets me jobs."
—actor Steve Buscemi

Less popular kids tend to be perceived as different, or unconventional. This can be a really good thing. Being unconventional means that you are original and an individual. The world thrives on unconventional people. They grow up to be the inventors, artists, and visionaries of this world.

The other thing about popularity is that it usually doesn't last forever. If you're not popular now, it doesn't mean that it's always going to be that way. Many kids who feel like outsiders grow up to be extremely happy and successful people. And a lot of popular kids grow up to be nothing like the big shots they were when they were younger.

>>Cliques<<

A clique is a tight-knit group of friends who usually consider themselves something of an exclusive club. All schools have cliques.

Kids in cliques typically have something in common that brings them together, such as an activity or a lifestyle. Cliques often have unofficial "uniforms"—whether it's torn jeans and leather jackets, mohawks and pierced eyebrows, or expensive designer duds. Athletes, or "jocks," for example, form a clique at some schools. Guys who are into computers are sometimes lumped together too. Kids who are into a certain kind of music and look may make up another.

Because they tend to be exclusive, cliques can be a drag. Although the kids in them might be cool as individuals, as a group, cliques can sometimes be pretty cruel. Cliques might look down upon or dis kids who aren't part of their group. And there's nothing that hurts more than being excluded.

It's natural to want to fit in, but the attempt can be painful. You shouldn't have to change who you are just to be part of a group. If joining a group means doing things you're uncomfortable with, don't join that group. If you have to pick on other kids to belong, you should try to fit into some other group. If you have to transform yourself to be accepted into a clique, that means the kids in the clique don't really want you in their group—they want a photocopy of themselves.

Who Am I?

5 <<<Pals and Parents>>>

Before you hit double digits in age, your parents were probably the most important people in your life. Your parents will continue to have a big influence on you and on the decisions you make.

As you move into the middle school years and your early teens, most likely this will change. You'll become more independent and start spending more time with your pals. This can be tricky for both you and your folks.

>>Juggling Friends and Family<<

As friends become more important parts of your life, you may find yourself running into new conflicts with your parents. It might seem as if your parents are constantly on your case just because you want to hang out with your buds. Maybe your parents are having difficulty adapting to the fact that you're not at home as much.

Like everyone, you have rights and responsibilities. You have the right to your own life and your own friends, but you also have responsi-bilities as a mem-ber of your family. If your mom asks you to take out the garbage or your dad asks you to baby-sit your little sister, don't just say, "No, I'm going out with the

guys" and walk out the door. Aside from helping around the house, there are simple little things you can do to keep things smooth between you and your parents. Things like letting them know where you'll be, with whom, and around what time you plan to come home. Things like not missing your curfew. Things like calling your parents and letting them know if you're going to miss or be late for dinner. (Although this always happens, don't wait until fifteen minutes before dinnertime to call. The effect will be the same as if you hadn't called at all: lots of screeching!)

These fundamentals of family life do more than keep your parents off your case. They help keep you safe. The simple fact is that no matter how old you get, someone should know where you are. I know: You're growing up now, and you can take care of yourself. It's not as if you have to tell your parents absolutely everything about your private life. But if you keep them informed of the basics, everybody will be a lot happier.

>>When Parents Don't Like Your Pals<<

It's only normal that parents will want to meet your friends. They're interested in your life and care about whom you hang out with. Your parents don't have the right to choose your friends for you, but because you live with them, they have a right to know who your pals are.

Your parents will probably like and approve of most of your pals. However, there are bound to be one or two whom they don't. Maybe your parents find a certain friend rude and unfriendly. Could this opinion be true? Maybe your friend is shy or uncomfortable around adults. If so, maybe he'll loosen up after spending a little more time with your folks.

Your parents might think that one of your pals seems like a troublemaker who could get you into hot water. Ask them why they think this is so. Maybe your buddy comes off as kind of scary with his pierced tongue, his shocking blue hair, and his German army boots. If you think that they're unfairly judging a book by its cover, talk to them. Your parents will probably loosen up if they spend a little more time with your pal and learn what's beneath his brilliant blue 'do.

On the other hand, maybe your parents see aspects of your friend that you don't see. Ask them why they think that he might be a bad influence on you. Do you think they're justified? If you don't, explain why, but keep an open mind. Tell them that you'll be careful and keep your eyes open, and if their suspicions are correct, you'll distance yourself from that person. Hopefully if you're open with them and respect their point of view, they'll trust you to do the right thing.

5 <<<Girl Friends, Not Girlfriends>>>

You have probably gone through a stage where you and your buds are not into girls too much. You may still feel that way. You might think that they're irritating, annoying, or royal pains in the butt.

At some point in middle school, your feelings will probably start to change. You and your pals might start getting interested in girls in a romantic or sexual way. You might start checking girls out, talking about them as possible girlfriend material, even flirting a little.

If you're really smart, however, you'll catch on to the very true fact that girls make excellent friends. If you count only guys among your best buds, you're missing out.

>>Why Girls Make Good Friends<<

There are quite a few reasons why girls make good friends. First of all, they tend to be more open and more communicative than guys. They're great to talk to and are good listeners. Usually you can cut the crap and forget the bravado that you might feel you have to keep up with the guys.

In general, with a friend of the opposite sex, you won't feel the same sense of competitiveness that you may feel with guys. For the same reason, girls can give you a whole different perspective on many subjects. In particular, they can give you the inside scoop on other girls.

Having lots of girls as friends will help you get along with and understand girls, and later women, throughout your life. Guys who never have any girl friends may have difficulty communicating and relating to women. They might end up scared or suspicious of them. Meanwhile, guys who have many girl friends will feel confident and comfortable with women and know how to relax and have fun hanging out with them.

>>Don't Listen to the Guys<<

Sometimes the toughest thing about being friends with a girl is other guys. They might tease you for hanging out with girls. Maybe they'll call you "girly" because you have a good time doing modern dance or singing in the choir with a group of girls. Or perhaps they'll get on your case, embarrassing you (and her) with constant ribbing about when you guys are going to "do something."

This is no reason for you to be self-conscious about being friends with girls. After all, are you going to let some other guys dictate whom you can and can't be friends with? Furthermore, you'll notice that it's only guys who don't have any girl friends of their own who get on your case. Maybe this is because deep down they're jealous of your ease with girls, whereas they are still insecure in the presence of the opposite sex.

>>"We're Just Friends"<<

Sometimes when you're friends with a girl, people around you will assume that she's your girlfriend instead of a friend who

is a girl. Not only peers but parents too might jump to such a conclusion.

From time to time, the frontier between "just friends" and romantic interest might blur a little. You might discover after being close friends that one or both of you have deeper feelings for each other.

If you start feeling more than just friendship for a girl who's a pal, make sure that she feels it too before you blurt out your emotions or make a move. If she doesn't share your feelings, you risk making both her and yourself uncomfortable. You could also jeopardize your friendship.

If you feel that your romantic feelings are mutual, try talking about them or acting upon them—but slowly and carefully. People act one way in a friendship and another way in a romantic relationship, and moving from one to another can be very delicate. A great friendship can last a really long time, so being "just friends" is a tremendous thing.

<<<Tough Times>>>

Whether it's a parent, sibling, or pal, when you have a close relationship with someone, it is normal that there will come a time when you disagree, fight, or don't get along. In fact, it would be weird if this never happened.

Like all relationships, friendships—even the closest ones—go through phases and change. This is especially true when you are young and both you and your life are changing a lot. Obviously it can be really upsetting to be in a fight or not to get along with a friend. Know that there are both positive and negative ways of dealing with tough times.

>>When Friends Fight<<

No two people are exactly alike. Everyone is different, with different needs, desires, and ways of seeing and handling things. Because of this there are always going to be moments of conflict in friendships. Some of these conflicts will result in arguments or fights.

Depending on the nature and intensity of the fight, and the personalities involved, you and your buddy will react in different ways when things get ugly.

Maybe you'll yell at each other and then apologize. Maybe your friend will insult you or tick you off. Perhaps you'll call him on it right away and let him know how you feel. Or perhaps after a period during which you're hurt or angry, you'll just decide that it's not important and let it go.

No matter what, everybody gets angry and loses control. It's better to air out problems than to let them simmer inside you. Ultimately there are two ways of dealing with an argument or disagreement: You can work it out or end the friendship.

Cool Quotes

"We have arguments, but we've never had a major bust-up with punches thrown or anything. We snap at each other, but we all know that it's due to tiredness and stress."
—Rich Neville of the band Five

>>Working Things Out<<

Disagreements can be complicated to work out in a way that satisfies both parties. Although no set rules exist, there are definitely good ways and bad ways of resolving conflict. Here are five good things to try:

1 Identify the real problem: Maybe your pal lashed out at you for no reason. Find out what the real deal is with him.

2 Put yourself in his shoes. Try to see your pal's point of view and not just your own.

3 Open up. Be honest about what's really bugging you.

4 Have good timing. Wait for the right moment for both of you to talk things out.

5 Be careful with your words. Think before you open your mouth. Maybe take some time and write your beefs down on paper. This will help you blow off steam and organize your thoughts.

Similarly, certain things are likely to make a disagreement with a friend even worse. Five things not to do include the following:

1. Resort to silent treatment. Giving your buddy the cold shoulder 'cause things don't go your way won't resolve anything. If your buddy asks you what the problem is, don't say "nothing" if something is wrong.

2. Blow up. Yelling, screaming, stomping, and punching won't solve anything.

3. Attack. Going for your pal's throat by letting him know his every fault and everything he's ever done wrong will make things much worse.

4. Run away. Don't just walk away instead of dealing with the problem. A lot of people are frightened by confrontation and disappear or withdraw into a shell at the first sign of trouble.

5. Act too proud. The "He started it, so it's up to him to come crawling back to me" attitude isn't going to get you anywhere.

>>When Friendships End<<

Some friendships will last for the rest of your life. Many others won't. As you get older and change, you might find that you and a close pal will no longer enjoy doing the same activities or have the same interests in common. Maybe one or both of you will change, and the result will be that you don't get along as well as you used to.

You might have a big fight about something and not be able to work it out. Or you might just slowly drift apart. Maybe your pal will get mixed up with a bad crowd, or maybe you'll move away to another city.

Regardless of what happens, occasionally it's impossible to fix things. And sometimes you don't even want to. Sometimes it's just time to call a friendship quits. Whether you talk about this directly or each quietly go your own way, it's always sad to lose a friend.

>>Conclusion: That's What Friends Are For<<

Friends can be weird, complicated, up-and-down, even down-and-out. They can also be the best thing that ever happened to you.

Take good care of your friends, and hopefully they'll take good care of you. Leave yourself open to new people and experiences, and you'll end up having an interesting life full of variety. Remember that you can make pals anywhere and anytime. You can have friends of every age, sex, nationality, and religion.

You can have a posse of pals, or a real close one-on-one buddy. Or both. You can also have more than one group of friends. Don't put limits on yourself or your friendships, because there is no limit to the number of different kinds of friends you can have.

Life can be pretty screwed up sometimes, and it really helps if you have a solid pal or 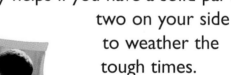 two on your side to weather the tough times.

 Life can also be a blast, and it can be all the more so if you have a buddy or two to share it with.

<<< What's the Word? >>>

addictive   Habit forming (as in drugs or alcohol).

bravado   A front or act of false bravery.

clique   An exclusive group of friends.

confrontation   To have it out with someone face-to-face.

conventional   Following the standard or norm.

extracurricular   Outside of school.

insecurity   Lack of self-confidence.

jeopardize   To put at risk.

mohawk   A haircut with a shaved scalp and a spiky ridge of hair in the center, popular with punks.

peers   People around you of your own age.

peer pressure   When companions try to persuade you to conform to their own standards of behavior.

quirky   Offbeat, unusual.

ritual   A ceremonial act.

scope   To check out (someone).

silent treatment   Giving someone the cold shoulder on purpose.

42

<<<It's a Guy's World>>>

Big Brothers and Sisters of America
230 North 13th Street
Philadelphia, PA 19107
(215) 567-7000
Web site: http://www.bbsa.org

Boy Scouts
Greater New York Council
345 Hudson Street
New York, NY 10014
(212) 242-1100
National Web site: http://www.bsa.scouting.org

Boys and Girls Club of America
771 First Avenue
New York, NY 10017
(212) 351-5900
Web site: http://www.bgca.org

Boys and Girls Club of Canada
7030 Woodbine Avenue, Suite 703
Markham, Ontario, L3R 6G2
(416) 477-7272

YMCA of the USA
101 North Wacker Drive
Chicago, IL 60606
Web site: http://www.ymca.net

YMCA of Canada
42 Charles Street East, 6th Floor
Toronto, Ontario M47 1T4
(416) 967-9622
Web site: http://www.ymca.ca

Web Sites

The Adolescence Directory On-Line
http://education.indiana.edu/cas/adol/adol.htm

Healthy Relationships
http://fox.nstn.ca/~healthy

Manhood Home Page
http://www.manhood.com.au

My Future
http://www.myfuture.com

Stop the Violence…Face the Music Society
http://www.stv.net

The Student School Change Network.
http://www.nmia.com/~sscn/

Youth Assistance Organization
http://www.youth.org/elight/

<<< By the Book >>>

Ambrose, Stephen E. *Comrades: Brothers, Fathers, Heroes, Sons, Pals.* New York: Simon & Schuster, 1999.

Covington, Dennis. *Lizard.* New York: Bantam Doubleday Dell, 1993.

Hinton, S.E. *The Outsiders.* New York: Puffin Books, 1997.

Marano, Hara Estroff. *Why Doesn't Anybody Like Me?* William Morrow, 1998.

McDonald, Joyce. *Swallowing Stones.* New York: Bantam Books, 1997.

Paulsen, Gary. *Hatchet.* New York: Aladdin Paperbacks, 1987.

Peck, Lee. *Coping with Cliques.* New York: Rosen Publishing Group, 1992.

Re, Judith. *Social Savvy: A Handbook for Teens.* New York: Simon and Schuster, 1992.

Roehm, Michelle, ed. *Boys Know It All: Wise Thoughts and Wacky Ideas from Guys Like You.* Hillsboro, OR: Beyond Words Publishing, 1998.

Salinger, J. D. *The Catcher in the Rye.* New York: Little, Brown & Co., 1951.

Spinelli, Jerry. *Wringer.* New York: HarperCollins, 1998.

Thomas, Rob. *Rats Saw God.* New York: Simon & Schuster, 1996.

<<< Index >>>

physical differences, 9
popularity, 23-25
problems, 7, 13, 37

R

responsibilities, 28, 29
rights, 28

S

secrets, 7
sex, 32, 33, 34, 41
sisters, 5, 29
sports, 11
studying, 11
style, 24

T

talking, 10, 33
teachers, 11

V

Van Der Beek, James, 17

<<< Credits >>>

About the author

Michael Sommers is a twin from Canada who lives in Brazil. He has a degree in psychology, an 18-year-old orange cat named Jesse in Toronto, and friends all around the world.

Photo credits

Cover photo © Ken Chernus/FPG; pp. 5, 29 © FPG; pp. 8, 13, 32, 40, 41 © International Stock; pp. 9, 36 © Shalhevet Moshe; p. 16 © Seth Dinnerman; pp. 23, 25 © Everett; p. 34 © Thaddeus Harden.

Series design

Oliver H. Rosenberg

Layout

Rebecca L. Stern

Consulting editor

Amy Haugesag